RYŌKAN
Zen Monk-Poet of Japan

Prepared for the Columbia College Program
of Translations from the Oriental Classics

RYŌKAN

Zen Monk-Poet
of Japan

Translated by
BURTON WATSON

NEW YORK
COLUMBIA UNIVERSITY PRESS

The Japan Foundation, through a special grant,
has assisted the Press in publishing this volume.

Library of Congress Cataloging in Publication Data

Ryōkan, 1758–1831.
  Ryōkan, Zen monk-poet of Japan.

  Consists chiefly of translations of selected Japanese and Chinese poems, the
former with romanized Japanese text in parallel columns.
  "Translations from the Oriental classics."
  I. Watson, Burton, 1925— II. Title
PL797.6.A29 1977   895.6'1'3   77-11140
ISBN 0-231-04414-3
ISBN 0-231-04415-1 (pbk.)

Columbia University Press
New York Guildford, Surrey

c 10 9 8 7 6 5 4 3 2 1
p 10 9 8 7 6 5 4 3 2 1

For Zenshin Ryufū
(Philip Whalen)

Translations From the Oriental Classics

Editorial Board

CONTENTS

INTRODUCTION

A MASTER CALLIGRAPHER, a writer of unusual and highly personal poetry in Japanese and Chinese, an eccentric holed up in a tiny mountain hut, a lanky, beak-nosed cleric begging for food or playing crazy games with the village children—these are some of the images summoned up by the name Ryōkan, a monk of the Sōtō branch of the Zen sect who lived in Japan in the late eighteenth and early nineteenth century. His works have long been loved and admired by his countrymen, one of whom predicted that the time would come when they would be appreciated in China and the West as well.[1] The present book is an attempt to fulfill part of that prophecy by presenting English translations of a selection of Ryōkan's poems in Japanese and Chinese, along with a brief prose work in Chinese.

Ryōkan was born in 1758 in the village of Izumozaki in Echigo province, present-day Niigata, on the northwest coast of the main island of Japan. His father had been adopted into the Yamamoto family of Izumozaki and held the posts hereditary in the family, those of *nanushi* or village headman, and custodian of the local Shinto shrine. He was also something of a haiku poet and went by the literary name I'nan. Ryōkan's mother came from another branch of the Yamamoto family living in the nearby island of Sado.

1. See the remarks by the eminent poet and critic Saitō Mokichi (1882–1953) quoted in Karaki Junzō, *Ryōkan*, Nihon shijinsen #20 (Tokyo: Chikuma shobō, 1971), pp. 229–30. Other outstanding men of modern Japanese letters who have expressed admiration for and indebtedness to Ryōkan's works include Masaoka Shiki, Natsume Sōseki, Takamura Kōtarō, and Kawabata Yasunari.

Ryōkan, who as a boy bore the name Eizō, attended a private school in the neighborhood run by a Confucian scholar, over a period of five or six years receiving a basic education in Chinese and Japanese. Because he was the eldest son, he then began training to succeed his father as village headman. In the summer of 1775, at the age of seventeen, however, apparently without his parents' permission, he abruptly entered a local temple of the Zen sect and began religious training. Some accounts say he shaved his head and became a monk immediately, adopting the religious name Ryōkan, others that he did not take this step until four years later. Meanwhile his younger brother Yoshiyuki replaced him as family heir.

Just what impelled Ryōkan to take this dramatic step is uncertain. Numerous legends and anecdotes have accumulated about his name, and these depict him as a sensitive, introspective, and bookish boy who by temperament might be expected to be drawn to the religious life. His family, whose fortunes were clearly on the decline, had many Buddhist connections, and a number of its members at one time or another entered the clergy. For Ryōkan, an eldest son, to do so, and in such a precipitate manner, however, was surely unconventional. Probably he found, in his period of apprenticeship as village headman, that he had no taste or aptitude for administrative affairs—there is a tale of his having bungled as mediator in a dispute between the local officials and the fishermen of the village, mainly because of the unfortunate frankness with which he conveyed the contestants' opinions to one another. Anecdote suggests other motives to explain his sudden decision to enter religious life, among them an unhappy marriage, and shock at attending the beheading of a condemned criminal.

In 1779 the Zen master Kokusen, head of the Entsū-ji temple in Bitchū in present-day Okayama Prefecture, happened to pass through Echigo and stopped at the temple where Ryōkan was living. Ryōkan immediately determined to become his disciple and followed him back to the Entsū-ji, spending the next ten years or so in religious training under Kokusen's guidance. Eventually he gained full enlightenment and received *inka*, the sanction of his teacher to become a Zen master in his own right. After Kokusen's death in 1791, he left the Entsū-ji and spent some five years wandering about the country, though exactly where he went or how he lived is uncertain.

In 1795 Ryōkan's father visited Kyoto and, evidently out of disillusionment at the powerless situation of the imperial family, drowned himself in the Katsura River, though some accounts say the suicide was feigned and that in fact he withdrew to the great Buddhist center at Mount Kōya on the Kii Peninsula. Ryōkan somehow received word of the event and went to Kyoto to attend memorial services for his father, after which he returned to his native region, where he remained for the rest of his life.

Ryōkan stayed at a number of temples and lodgings in the area, and around 1804 settled down in the Gogō-an or Five Measures of Rice Retreat, a little one-room hut on the slopes of Mount Kugami that belonged to a temple at the top of the mountain.[2] He remained there for the following thirteen years. When age made it difficult for him to hike up and down the trail, he moved to the grounds of the Otogo Shinto shrine at

2. The name Gogō-an was not given to the hut by Ryōkan but by a monk who had lived there previously and received a daily ration of five *gō*, or measures of rice, from the temple. Ryōkan, it should be noted, received no such ration.

the foot of the mountain, and later to a renovated storehouse at the home of a friend in the village of Shimazaki. He died there in 1831 at the age of seventy-three.

Unlike most distinguished Japanese Buddhist priests, Ryōkan never headed a temple of his own. Instead, he chose to live alone, simply, frugally, and independently, devoting his time to meditation, literary pursuits, and *takuhatsu*, the begging expeditions to nearby villages and towns by which he supported himself. Because of these expeditions he became a familiar figure in the neighborhood, and seems to have been particularly popular among the children, with whom he romped and played in a markedly unsanctimonious manner.

Some of the games he played are described in his poems. In addition to these, anecdote relates that he used to lie down and pretend to be dead while the children gleefully buried him in dry leaves.

He exchanged poems and visited back and forth with his brother Yoshiyuki and other relatives and with a number of literary-minded friends in the region. Best known of such literary friendships was that which he struck up around 1826, when he was sixty-eight, with a Zen Buddhist nun named Teishin (1798–1872), forty years his junior. Teishin, attracted to him both as a poet and as a man of religion, visited him often at the renovated storehouse in Shimazaki where he was living at the time, and the two exchanged numerous poems giving expression to their deep though wholly platonic affection for one another. These and other Japanese poems by Ryōkan were later collected by Teishin in a work entitled *Hachisu no tsuyu* or *Lotus Dew* (preface dated 1835), which constitutes an important source on his final years.

Ryōkan had at least one religious disciple, a layman named Miwa Saichi, who died in 1807. Ryōkan was deeply grieved by his death and thereafter apparently made little or no effort to pass on to others his understanding of the profounder principles of Zen. Thus he died without leaving any Dharma heir or successor to his teachings. Far from pressing his own brand of Buddhism upon others, he repeatedly stressed the essential unity of all Buddhist teaching. And when writing poems for friends who belonged to the Shin sect, the prevalent form of Buddhism in the region, he extolled such practices as the recitation of the *Namu Amida Butsu* formula and the faith in the Western Paradise of the Buddha Amida, which the Shin sect preached. His religious name, Ryōkan, means "Goodly Tolerance," and he evidently took it seriously. A second religious name that he adopted, Taigu or "Great Fool," also appears to reflect his image of himself. In his youth he was known among the villagers as a *hiru-andon*, a person who is as pointless and ineffectual as "a lamp at midday." By dubbing himself "Great Fool," he showed that he gave ready assent to their opinion.

The seacoast where Ryōkan lived is noted for its heavy snows and he was often snowed in in winter, particularly when he lived on Mount Kugami. During such periods he passed the time by poring over works of Japanese and Chinese poetry, particularly the poems of the T'ang dynasty Buddhist recluse Han-shan, the Master of Cold Mountain. In Japanese literature his favorite was the *Man'yōshū*, the great anthology of ancient poetry compiled in the eighth century, which he read assiduously and imitated in his own works, and from which he compiled a little selection of particular favorites. When the weather permitted, however, he foraged over the hills for firewood or edible greens, busied himself with chores about his hut, or left the mountain to play with his beloved children friends and mingle with the villagers. His poems and the accounts of him left by his contemporaries make it clear that, though rather shy and awkward, he was a man of great warmth and compassion, by no means the kind who entirely shuts himself off from society.

It is characteristic of Ryōkan that he compiled no collection of his poems, at least of those in Japanese, but was content merely to scatter them about among his friends and acquaintances.[3] When his fame as a poet and calligrapher grew in later years, he was often pressed for samples of his work, and seems to have complied good-naturedly, writing out a version of one of his earlier compositions if he could not come up with an original poem for the occasion. As a result, many of his poems have come to exist in a number of slightly different versions. Teishin was the first to put together a collection of his poems in Japanese, the work noted above, and this was followed in time by other collections. Fortunately for posterity, Ryōkan was so revered as a man and admired as a poet and calligrapher that the persons to whom he gave his works were careful to preserve them. By rummaging through the storehouses of families in the area, scholars have so far succeeded in recovering some 1,400 poems in Japanese and over 450 in Chinese, as well as letters and other writings, and it is possible that further search will in time enlarge the corpus.

Ryōkan's *waka* or poetry in Japanese employs three forms: the *tanka*, a thirty-one-syllable poem arranged in five lines in a 5-7-5-7-7 pattern; the *sedōka*, a poem in six lines in 5-7-7-5-7-7 pattern; and the *chōka*, a form of unlimited length that employs alternating lines of five and seven syllables and ends

3. He evidently did compile a brief collection of his works in Chinese, the *Sōdōshū* or *Grass Hall Collection*, but it contains only a fraction of his Chinese poems.

with an extra seven-syllable line, often followed by one or more envoys in *tanka* form. These are the three forms represented in the *Man'yōshū*, which Ryōkan so highly admired, and it is not surprising that he should have tried his hand at all of them.

The *tanka* became the dominant poetic form in the centuries following the compilation of the *Man'yōshū*, but the *sedōka* and *chōka* dropped almost entirely out of use, the latter probably because it is so difficult to handle effectively. There was a great resurgence of interest in the *Man'yōshū* and other classics of ancient Japanese literature in the eighteenth century, which inspired sporadic efforts to revive the *chōka* form. Ryōkan's *sedōka* and *chōka*, though less numerous than his *tanka*, represent interesting and at times remarkably successful attempts to bring new life to these long neglected forms.

Ryōkan's Japanese poetry shows the influence of the twelfth-century priest-poet Saigyō, but the *Man'yōshū* clearly constituted his chief model. The *Man'yōshū*, because of its antiquity and the peculiar graphic system in which it is recorded, abounds in problems of reading and interpretation, many of which had not been solved in Ryōkan's time and indeed to some extent remain unsolved today. Because he studied the work on his own rather than under the tutelage of an expert, he no doubt read the text imperfectly and with difficulty.[4] Nevertheless he believed that, even imperfectly understood, it constituted the surest guide in matters of Japanese poetry. He was willing to admit the worth of the *Kokinshū*,

4. He appears to have relied mainly upon the *Man'yōshū ryakuge*, a popular commentary completed by Tachibana Chikage in 1796 and printed in 1812.

the next important anthology, compiled around 905, but he appears to have had little use for the numerous anthologies produced thereafter.[5]

Ryōkan often, particularly in his *chōka*, imitated the actual language of the *Man'yōshū*, which means that he employed a deliberately archaic style and diction. He also, like his model, made frequent use of *makura-kotoba*, or "pillow-words," conventionalized epithets attached to certain words to lend sonority to the poem.[6] But what he seems to have esteemed most in the anthology and tried hardest to capture in his own work is its spirit of simplicity and openness, its freedom from literary artifice and intellectualization. Thus, although he often borrowed its diction, he employed such diction, as the *Man'yōshū* poets themselves had done, to record the actual scenes and experiences of his own daily life. The combination of archaic language and highly realistic and contemporary content that results may appear peculiar—rather as though a poet of Wordsworth's time and temperament had written in the language of Spenser. But it is representative of a phenomenon recurrent in both Japanese and Chinese literature, the effort to achieve innovation through a return to the finest works and ideals of the past. That the combination, odd though it may be, succeeds brilliantly in literary terms is attested by the critical acclaim which Ryōkan's poems have enjoyed over the years since their appearance and the fact that his reputation continues to grow.

The Japanese at many periods in their history have been en-

5. See his remarks quoted in Tōgō Toyoharu, *Ryōkan kashū* (Osaka: Sōgensha, 1963), p. 388.

6. Because the *makura-kotoba* are often obscure in meaning or close to meaningless, they are a bane to the translator, who is never certain how or to what degree he should attempt to bring them over in translation. I have in many cases not tried to represent them in English.

thusiastic writers of poetry and prose in Chinese as well as in their native language. The Zen monks of the thirteenth, fourteenth, and fifteenth centuries produced an important body of works in Chinese known as *Gozan bungaku*, the "Literature of the Five Mountains," as the major Zen temples of Kamakura and Kyoto were known. In the Edo period, which began in 1600, the government's encouragement of Confucianism led many Japanese to take up the study of Chinese language and literature, bringing about a revival of interest in the writing of *kanshi* or poetry in Chinese. Ryōkan lived just at the time when an earlier infatuation with T'ang poetry was giving way to a taste for the more homey and realistic works of the Sung, and when the *kanshi* form was being adapted to Japanese tastes and themes and enjoying a popularity quite unknown in the past. For these reasons, and because he was a follower of the Zen sect, which places great emphasis upon the doctrinal importance of Chinese verse and the works of certain Chinese poets such as Han-shan and Su Tung-p'o, it is not surprising that he should have written poetry in Chinese.

As in the case of his poetry in Japanese, Ryōkan did not ally himself with any contemporary school or teacher of *kanshi*, but worked quite on his own, turning directly to the works he most admired, the early classics of Chinese poetry and the T'ang masters, particularly Han-shan, for inspiration.

Han-shan, whose dates are unknown but who probably lived in the late eighth and early ninth century, was a layman follower of Zen Buddhism who retired to a place called Cold Mountain in the T'ien-t'ai mountain range of Chekiang. The poems attributed to him, some three hundred, are untitled, generally quite short, and cast in simple, often colloquial language. Some are satires on the follies of the world or sermons on Buddhist practice and belief, others descriptions of the rugged mountain scenery of the poet's retreat and of the austere but unfettered life he lived there.

Ryōkan sometimes produced imitations of specific poems in the Han-shan collection, particularly the satires. But more often he adapted Han-shan's simplicity of language and directness of approach in depicting the experiences of his own life. Like his poems in Japanese, his *kanshi* are thus mainly a record of his year-round activities—the snowbound winter nights in his hut, the begging expeditions to towns and villages, the games he played with the children, his journeys and visits with friends—along with a certain number of works of a specifically doctrinal nature. He rails less at the world than does Han-shan—when he rails, it is usually at his fellow monks—and his physical and spiritual withdrawal from society was far less drastic and unconditional. For this reason, and because we know much more about his life, he comes across in his poetry as a warmer and more approachable person than Han-shan, though equally eccentric in his own way.

One other characteristic of Ryōkan's *kanshi* makes them distinctively his own. This is the fact that he often violates the prosodic requirements of Chinese verse, at times using rhymes that are faulty or no rhymes at all, ignoring considerations of tonal parallelism, and employing patterns of diction and syntax that, though intelligible, are quite unconventional. Japanese *kanshi* are never recited aloud in Chinese pronunciation, but are transposed into Japanese in accordance with a set of conventions, and thus the rhymes and other formal features of the poem become wholly obscured in recitation. Nevertheless, Japanese have generally felt that if one elects to write in Chinese forms, one should abide by the rules laid down for them by the Chinese. Ryōkan's failure to do so has obliged critics to describe his *kanshi* euphemistically as "in a class by themselves." Ryōkan no doubt anticipated such a judgment when he wrote the following verse:

Who says my poems are poems?
My poems are not poems at all!
Only when you understand that my poems are not poems
can we begin to talk about poems.[7]

As this suggests, Ryōkan went very much his own way, not only in his *kanshi* but in his Japanese poetry as well, and indeed in his whole manner of life. Unlike most eminent scholars, artists, and writers of the Edo period, he was allied with no particular school or line of filiation, and for that reason I have not tried to discuss him in terms of the intellectual and literary currents of the time. He was by no means self-taught but undoubtedly had his teachers and others who influenced him in his spiritual and artistic development. In the end, however, his highly individual character and talent led him in directions quite different from those of his contemporaries. He belongs in a sense less to his own age than to the ages that followed, which discovered his work, responded to it with enthusiasm, and made it a part of the mainstream of Japanese literary tradition in a way it had not been at the time of its appearance. Today he is recognized as one of the greatest figures of late Edo period literature, a man who, as I have noted, seems to increase in stature with the years. He is one of those rare writers who, perhaps because of his innovations and unconventionality, appears to speak even more commandingly to posterity than he did to his own age.

My selection consists of translations of forty-three of Ryōkan's poems in Chinese and eighty-three of those in Jap-

7. Tōgō Toyoharu, *Ryōkan shishū* (Osaka: Sōgensha, 1962), p. 134.

anese; the latter include seventy-four *tanka,* eight *chōka,* and one *sedōka.*[8] The number prefixed to the translation indicates the number of the poem in two works by Tōgō Toyoharu, *Ryōkan shishū* (Osaka: Sōgensha, 1962) for the poems in Chinese, and *Ryōkan kashū* (Osaka: Sōgensha, 1963) for the poems in Japanese, though in the case of the latter I sometimes follow a slightly different version of the text. The originals of the Japanese poems are given in romanized form, since poetry in classical Japanese is quite intelligible in such form; poetry in Chinese, however, is not, hence no originals are included for the poems in Chinese. My selection concludes with excerpts from Ryōkan's list of ninety "Admonitory Words," written in Japanese, and a prose piece in Chinese, the *Shōjujiki-mon* or "Statement on Begging for Food," in which he discusses the Buddhist practice of begging for alms from the populace.

A few of Ryōkan's *kanshi* appear to date from his days at the Entsū-ji, though most are from his later years. His Japanese poetry seems to date almost entirely from the period after his return to Echigo. Some critics claim to discern a certain stylistic development in his writing—an early austerity, followed by a growing mellowness and warmth. Since so few of his poems can be dated accurately, however, such attempts to delineate stylistic growth seem to be tenuous at best. My selections are grouped mainly by theme, with a number of the Japanese poems arranged in the form of a year-round cycle, though they were undoubtedly written over a period of years. A few poems that clearly belong to the close of his life have

---

8. Ryōkan also wrote haiku, of which the following Zen-flavored example is particularly famous:

Ura wo mise	Showing their faces
omote wo misete	showing their back sides
chiru momiji	the autumn leaves fall

been placed toward the end of the selection. As will be noted, most of his poems are untitled.

In addition to the works by Tōgō Toyoharu cited above, I have also consulted the sections dealing with Ryōkan by Yoshino Hideo and others in *Sanetomo shū, Saigyō shū, Ryōkan shū,* Koten Nihon bungaku zenshū #21 (Tokyo: Chikuma shobō, 1971); Karaki Junzō, *Ryōkan,* Nihon shijinsen #20 (Chikuma shobō, 1971); Watanabe Hideei, *Ryōkan shishū* (Tokyo: Mokujisha, 1974), and *Ryōkan shukke kō* (Niigata: Kōkodō shoten, 1974), also by Watanabe. It may be noted that the Ryōkan section of the first item mentioned above has recently been reprinted as a separate volume, Yoshino Hideo, *Ryōkan: uta to shōgai,* Chikuma sōsho #216 (Chikuma shobō, 1975).

A selection of Ryōkan's poetry in English translation, *Ryōkan the Great Fool* by Kodama Misao and Yanagishima Hikosaku, was published by the Kyoto Seika Junior College Press, Kyoto, 1969. A few of Ryōkan's Japanese poems are also translated in Donald Keene, ed., *Anthology of Japanese Literature* (New York: Grove Press, 1955); and Geoffrey Bownas and Anthony Thwaite, trs., *The Penguin Book of Japanese Verse* (Penguin Books, 1964). Some of my translations have appeared earlier in my *Japanese Literature in Chinese,* Vol. 2 (New York: Columbia University Press, 1976), *Antioch Review,* and *Montemora.*

WAKA: Poems in Japanese

[84]

Kusa makura	Though travels
yogoto ni kawaru	take me to
yadori ni mo	a different stopping place each night
musubu wa onaji	the dream I dream is always
furusato no yume	that same one of home

[869]

Yūgure ni	In twilight
Kugami no yama wo	crossing over
koekureba	Mount Kugami
takane ni shika no	at the crest I heard
koe wo kiki keri	the cry of a deer

[185]

Uzumibi ni
ashi sashikubete
fuseredomo
koyoi no samusa
hara ni tōrinu

Though I lie here
legs snuggled
close to the embers
tonight's cold
goes right through my stomach

[173]

Yama kage no
kusa no ihori wa
ito samushi
shiba wo takitsutsu
yo wo akashitemu

In the mountain's shadow
my grass hut's
so cold
I'll be up burning firewood
all night long

[909]

Ashihiki no   On slopes
Kugami no yama no   of Mount Kugami
fuyugomori   holed up for winter—
hi ni hi ni yuki no   day after day the snow
furu nabe ni   goes on falling
yukiki no michi no   till trails show no sign
ato mo tae   of a soul passing by
furusato hito no   and no word comes
oto mo nashi   from people at home:
ukiyo wo koko ni   so I shut my gate
kado sashite   on the drifting world
Hida no takumi ga   and here with this one thread
utsu nawa no   of clear water from the crags,
tada hitosuji no   straight as the string
iwa shimizu   plucked by the carpenters of Hida,
so wo inochi ni te   I keep myself alive
aratama no ʹ   through another year,
kotoshi no kyō mo   another today
kurashitsuru ka mo   I go on living

[1041]

Ashihiki no
iwama wo tsutau
koke mizu no
kasuka ni ware wa
sumiwataru ka mo

Faint trickle of
mossy water from
a crevice in the mountain rock:
the clear still way
I pass through the world

[209]

Ima yori wa
tsugite shirayuki
tsumoru rashi
michi fumiwakete
tare ka tou beki

From now on
white snow I know will
go on piling up—
who'd come tramping through it
to call on me?

[277]

Miyamabi ni
fuyugomori suru
oi no mi wo
tare ka towamashi
kimi naranaku ni

Deep in the mountains
an old man
holed up for winter—
who'd come to see me?
Who but you, friend!

[279]

Yomosugara
kusa no ihori ni
shiba taite
katarishi koto wo
itsu ka wasuremu

All through the night
in my grass hut
burning brushwood,
how we talked on and on—
when will I forget it?

[521]

Kaze maze ni	Mingling with the wind
yuki wa furikinu	the snow comes falling;
yuki maze ni	mingling with the snow
kaze wa fukikinu	the wind comes blowing;
uzumibi ni	by banked coals
ashi sashinobete	I stretch my legs,
tsurezure to	idle, idle,
kusa no ihori ni	in this grass hut
tojikomori	a shut-in,
uchikazoureba	and counting, find
kisaragi mo	that the second month too
yume no gotoku ni	like a dream
sugi ni kerashimo	has come and gone

Waking from a Dream of Yoshiyuki

(the poet's younger brother)

[434]

Izuku yori	Where did you come from,
yoru no yumeji wo	following dream paths
tadori koshi	through the night to reach me,
miyama wa imada	these deep mountains
yuki no fukaki ni	still heaped high with snow?

(Sent to Yoshiyuki)

[433]

Ika ni shite	I wonder how
kimi imasuramu	you're making out—
kono goro no	spring thaw
yukige no kaze no	and the wind these days
hibi ni samuki ni	blowing so cold!

(Sent in thanks to Yoshiyuki)

[455]

Shikishima no	Land of Yamato,
Yamato no kuni wa	island-strewn,
inishie yu	from times past a land where
kotoage senu kuni	they do not lift up words; [1]
shikaredomo	nevertheless
ware wa kotoage su	I will lift up these words.
Sugishi natsu	Last summer, a gift
oto no tamaishi	from my little brother—
tsukuri kawa	a piece of tanned leather
iya tōjiroku	white and clean
tae no ho ni	as tapa cloth,
arinishi kawa ya	this leather
waga ie no	I look on
takara to omoi	as the treasure of my house—
yuku toki wa	I wrap it round me
oite motarashi	when I venture abroad,
neru toki wa	make it my coverlet
fusuma to nashite	when I go to bed,
tsuka no ma mo	never a moment
agami wo sarazu	parted from my side.
motarisedo	Since I've had it
kushiki shirushi mo	it's shown
ichijiruku	no special wonder,
arazari kereba	yet now I begin

---

1. To "lift up words" means to make special mention of or to praise. The opening passage imitates *Man'yōshū* XIII, nos. 3250 and 3253.

kono tabi wa	to consider
fukaku kōgae	more carefully,
kotosara ni	this time
yoru no koromo no	spread it over
ue ni shite	my sleeping pallet,
soga ue ni	try lying down
waga hada tsukete	to rest
fushinureba	right on top of it—
yoru wa sugara ni	and find I sleep soundly
umai shite	all night long,
honori honori to	warm and basky
mafuyuzuki	in dead-of-winter months,
harubi ni mukau	snug as though
kokochi koso sure	I were welcoming spring days!

[169]

Kusa no iho ni
nezamete kikeba
hisakata no
arare tobashiru
kuretake no ue ni

In my grass hut
I wake to hear
showers of hail
rattling over
the grove of bamboo

[563]

Asa na tsumu
shizuga kadota no
ta no aze ni
chikiri naku nari
haru ni wa narinu

Picking morning greens
in skimpy rows
of my kitchen garden
I hear a wagtail singing—
spring's really here!

[569]

Muragimo no	My heart
kokoro tanoshimo	is happy
haru no hi ni	on a spring day
tori no muragari	when I see the birds
asobu wo mireba	flocking together, playing

[19]

Kodomora yo	Children!
iza ide inamu	shall we be going now
Iyahiko no	to the hill
oka no sumire no	of Iyahiko
hana nioi mi ni	to see how the violets are blooming?

[2]

Kasumi tatsu
nagaki haru hi wo
kodomora to
temari tsukitsutsu
kono hi kurashitsu

Long spring days
when mists rise—
hitting the handball
along with the children
I've passed this one too.

[25]

Michi no be no
sumire tsumitsutsu
hachi no ko wo
wasurete zo koshi
sono hachi no ko wo

Picking violets
by the roadside
I've forgotten and left
my begging bowl—
that begging bowl of mine

[26]

Hachi no ko wo
waga wasururedomo
toru hito wa nashi
toru hito wa nashi
hachi no ko aware

I've forgotten
my begging bowl
but no one would steal it
no one would steal it—
how sad for my begging bowl

[621]

Hachi no ko ni
sumire tampopo
kokimazete
miyo no hotoke ni
tatematsuritena

In my begging bowl
violets and dandelions
jumbled together—
I offer them to the
Buddhas of the Three Worlds

[646]

Kusa no iho ni
ashi sashinobete
oyamada no
kawazu no koe wo
kikakushi yoshi mo

How pleasant—
in my grass hut
stretching out my legs
listening to the sound
of frogs in mountain paddies

[626]

Sanae toru
yamada no oda no
otomego ga
uchiaguru uta no
koe no harukesa

In paddies among the mountains
girls transplant
rice seedlings—
the sound of their singing
drifts up from far away

[410]

Kawazu naku	In fields
nobe no yamabuki	where frogs sing
taoritsutsu	I pick kerria roses
sake ni ukabete	float them on the wine—
tanoshiki wo tsume	have all the fun you can!

[711]

Waga yado no	On leaves of the plantain
nokiba ni ueshi	growing by the eaves
bashōha ni	of my hut
tsuki wa utsurinu	moonlight shines,
yo wa fukenu rashi	the night by now far gone

[669]

Natsu yama wo
waga koekureba
hototogisu
konure tachikuki
naki habuku miyu

As I cross the summer hills
I see a cuckoo
dart through treetops
beating his wings
and singing

[672]

Mizutori no
kamo no hairo no
aoyama no
konure sarazute
naku hototogisu

On green hills
the hue of
the water duck's wing,
a cuckoo lingers
singing in the treetops

[150]

Yūgiri ni
ochi no satobe wa
uzumorenu
sugi tatsu yado ni
kaerusa no michi

The distant village
lost in evening mist
when I make my way
home to my lodge
where cedars stand

[177]

Satobe ni wa
fue ya tsuzumi no
oto su nari
miyama wa sawa ni
matsu no oto shite

Down in the village
the din of
flute and drum,
here deep in the mountain
everywhere the sound of the pines

[282]

Koyoi ai
asu wa yamaji wo
hedatenaba
hitori yasumamu
moto no ihori ni

Tonight we meet,
tomorrow the
mountain path will part us,
and I'll lie down alone
in my same old hut

[37]

Ii kou to
waga kite mireba
hagi no hana
migiri shimimi ni
saki ni kerashimo

I came
to beg rice—
and find bush clover
blooming
all over the eave stones

[756]

Waga machishi
aki wa kinu rashi
kono yūbe
kusa mura goto ni
mushi no koe suru

The autumn I waited for
it seems has come—
this evening
from every clump of grass,
insect cries

[118]

Mizu ya kumamu
tatagi ya koramu
na ya tsumamu
asa no shigure no
furanu sono ma ni

Water to draw
brushwood to cut
greens to pick—
all in moments when
morning showers let up

[23]

Aki no ame no
harema ni idete
kodomora to
yamaji tadoreba
mo no suso nurenu

In a spell
when autumn rains let up
I went with the children,
following a mountain trail,
got the bottom of my robe all wet

[826]

Nani to naku
ura kanashiki wa
waga kado no
inaba soyogasu
hatsuaki no kaze

No reason,
yet it makes me sad—
by my door
the first fall winds
rustling through rice stalks

[153]

Yuku aki no
aware wo tare ni
kataramashi
akaza ko ni irete
kaeru yūgure

The sadness
of this passing autumn—
who to talk it out with?
a basket of wild spinach picked,
heading home at twilight

[305]

Tsukiyomi no
hikari wo machite
kaerimase
yamaji wa kuri no
iga no ōki ni

Wait for moonlight
before you try
to go home—
the mountain trail's
so thick with chestnut burs!

[740]

Aki mo yaya
yosamu ni narinu
waga kado ni
tsuzuresase chō
mushi no koe suru

Autumn, and nights
have grown bit by bit colder—
time to mend tatters!
say insect voices
by my door

[748]

Akikaze no
hi ni hi ni samuku
naru nabe ni
tomoshiku narinu
kirigirisu no koe

Autumn wind
day by day
blows colder,
cries of the crickets
each time feebler than before[1]

1. Ryōkan's poem, though very different in wording, recalls that of the twelfth-century priest-poet Saigyō:

Kirigirisu
yosamu ni aki no
naru mama ni
yowaru ka koe no
tōzakari yuku

Crickets—
as the cold of night
deepens into autumn
are you weakening? your voices
grow farther and farther away

[820]

Aki no nu no
kusa mura goto ni
oku tsuyu wa
yomosugara naku
mushi no namida ka

In the autumn meadow
dew that clings
to each clump of grass—
is it the tears of the insects
that cried all night long?

[306]

Tsuyu wa okinu
yamaji wa samushi
tachizake wo
oshite kaeraba
kedashi ikaga aramu

Dew on it,
the mountain trail will be cold—
before you head home
how about
a last drink of sake?

[122]

Hito towaba
Otogo no mori no
ko no shita ni
ochiba hiroite
iru to kotaeyo

If anyone asks
say I'm in the grove
of Otogo Shrine
picking up fallen leaves
under the trees

Taking Leave of Mount Kugami

(Probably written in 1826, when Ryōkan left his hut in the Otogo Shrine at the foot of Mt. Kugami and moved to the village of Shimazaki.)

[93]

Ashihiki no	Slopes
Kugami no yama no	of Mount Kugami—
yama kage no	in the mountain's shade
mori no shitaya ni	a hut beneath the trees—
iku toshi ka	how many years
waga suminishi wo	it's been my home?
karakoromo	The time comes
tachite shi kureba	to take leave of it—
natsugusa no	my thoughts wilt
omoi shinaete	like summer grasses,
yūzutsu no	I wander back and forth
ka yuki kaku yuki	like the evening star—
sono iho no	till that hut of mine
ikakuru made	is hidden from sight,
sono mori no	till that grove of trees
miezu naru made	can no longer be seen,
tamahoko no	at each bend
michi no kuma goto	of the long road,
kuma mo ochizu	at every turning,
kaerimi zo suru	I turn to look back
sono yama no be wo	in the direction of that mountain

[44]

Tarachine no Memories of my mother:
haha ga katami to morning and evening
asa yū ni I look
Sado no shimabe wo far off at those
uchimitsuru ka mo island shores of Sado [1]

[45]

Inishie ni The only things
kawaranu mono wa unchanged from the past:
Arisomi to the sea of Ariso
mukai ni miyuru and in sight beyond it
Sado no shima nari Sado Island

1. An island in sight off the coast of Echigo; Ryōkan's mother was born there.

White Hair

[1129]

Yoi yoi ni
shimo wa okedomo
yoshie yashi
asahi ni tokenu
toshi no ha ni
yuki wa furedomo
yoshie yashi
haruhi ni kienu
shikasuga ni
hito no kashira ni
furitsumeba
tsumi koso masare
aratama no
toshi wa furedomo
kiyu to iwanaku ni

Though frosts come down
night after night,
what does it matter?
they melt in the morning sun.
Though the snow falls
each passing year,
what does it matter?
with spring days it thaws.
Yet once let them settle
on a man's head,
fall and pile up,
go on piling up—
then the new year
may come and go,
but never you'll see them fade away

(Written on looking at little birds in a cage)

[1074]

Ori ori wa
miyama no negura
koinu beshi
ware mo mukashi no
omoyuraku ni

Now and then
you must long for your old nest
in the deep mountains—
I too have
memories of the past

On the Death of Saichi

(See p. 106)

[1139]

Kono sato no
yukiki no hito wa
amata aredo
kimi shi masaneba
sabishikari keri

In this village
coming and going
there're so many people—
but when you're not among them
it's lonely

(Written when he visited the house of a friend but found it deserted, with only a lone plum tree blooming in the garden)

[1064]

Ume no hana
oi ga kokoro wo
nagusameyo
mukashi no tomo wa
ima aranaku ni

Plum flowers,
comfort
an old man's heart!
My friend of past times
isn't here anymore

[1062]

Sono kami wa
sake ni uketsuru
ume no hana
tsuchi ni ochi keri
itazura ni shite

Plum flowers
that once we
floated on the wine—
now unheeded
fallen to the ground

(Two poems on a vase—1)

[492]

Inishie ni
ari kemu hito no
moteri chō
ōmiutsuwa wo
ware wa mochitari

Once owned,
they say, by
men of long ago,
this lovely vase—
and now it's mine!

(Two poems on a vase—2)

[486]

Ima yori wa
chiri wo mo sueji
asa na yū na
ware mihayasamu
itaku na wabi so

From now on not
a single speck of dust—
morning and night
I'll clean and care for you—
don't feel lonely!

The Rabbit in the Moon

(The poem is a retelling of one of the Jataka stories, tales of the Buddha in his earlier incarnations when he performed various acts of self-sacrifice. Ryōkan follows the version of the tale found in chapter five of the *Konjaku monogatari*, a collection of stories in Japanese, many Buddhist in nature, compiled around 1100. This version relates the Jataka tale to the old Chinese legend of a rabbit who inhabits the moon. There are numerous versions of the poem with slight textual variations; I follow the text given in Yoshino Hideo's collection, pp. 319–22.)

Isonokami	It took place in a world
furinishi miyo ni	long long ago
ari to iu	they say:
mashi to osagi to	a monkey, a rabbit,
kitsuni to ga	and a fox
tomo wo musubite	struck up a friendship,
ashita ni wa	mornings
nu yama ni asobi	frolicking field and hill,
yūbe ni wa	evenings
hayashi ni kaeri	coming home to the forest,
kaku shitsutsu	living thus
toshi no henureba	while the years went by,
hisakata no	when Indra,
Ame no Mikado no	sovereign of the skies,
kikimashite	hearing of this,
sore ga makoto wo	curious to know
shiramu to te	if it was true,
okina to narite	turned himself into an old man,
soga moto ni	tottering along,

yoroboi yukite	made his way to where they were.
mōsuraku	"You three,"
namutachi tagui wo	he said,
koto ni shite	"are of separate species,
onaji kokoro ni	yet I'm told play together
asobu chō	with a single heart.
makoto kikishi ga	If what I've heard
goto araba	is true,
okina ga ue wo	pray save an old man
sukue to te	who's hungry!"
tsue wo nagete	then he set his staff aside,
ikoi shi ni	sat down to rest.
yasuki koto to te	Simple enough, they said,
yaya arite	and presently
mashi wa ushiro no	the monkey appeared
hayashi yori	from the grove behind
ko no mi wo hiroite	bearing nuts
kitaritari	he'd gathered there,
kitsuni wa mae no	and the fox returned
ogawa yori	from the rivulet in front,
io wo kuwaete	clamped in his jaws
kitaritari	a fish he'd caught.
osagi wa atari ni	But the rabbit,
tobitobedo	though he hopped and hopped
	everywhere
nani mo mono sede	
arikereba	couldn't find anything at all,
osagi wa kokoro	while the others
koto nari to	cursed him because
nonoshirikereba	his heart was not like theirs.
hakanashi ya	Miserable me!
osagi hakarite	he thought
mōsuraku	and then he said,

mashi wa shiba wo	"Monkey, go cut me
karite koyo	firewood!
kitsuni wa kore wo	Fox, build me
yakite tabe	a fire with it!"
iu ga gotoku ni	and when they'd done
nashikereba	what he asked,
honoo no uchi ni	he flung himself
mi wo nagete	into the midst of the flames,
shiranu okina ni	made himself an offering
ataekeri	for an unknown old man.
okina wa kore wo	When the old man
miru yori mo	saw this
kokoro mo shinu ni	his heart withered.
hisakata no	He looked up to the sky,
ame wo aogite	cried aloud,
uchinakite	then sank to the ground,
tsuchi ni taurite	and in a while,
yaya arite	beating his breast,
mune uchitataki	said
mōsuraku	to the others,
namutachi mitari no	"Each of
tomodachi wa	you three friends
izure otoru to	has done his best,
nakeredomo	but what the rabbit did
osagi zo koto ni	touches me most!"
yasashi to te	Then he made the rabbit
moto no sugata ni	whole again
mi wo nashite	and gathering the dead body
kara wo kakaete	up in his arms,
hisakata no	took it and
tsuki no miya ni zo	laid it to rest
hōrikeru	in the palace of the moon.

ima no yo made mo	From that time till now
kataritsugi	the story's been told,
tsuki no usagi to	this tale
iu koto wa	of how the rabbit
kore ga yoshi ni te	came to be
ari keru to	in the moon,
kiku ware sae mo	and even I
shirotae no	when I hear it
koromo no sode wa	find the tears
tōrite nurenu	soaking the sleeve of my robe

[1031]

Sumizome no
waga koromode no
yuta naraba
ukiyo no tami wo
ōwamashi mono wo

If these sleeves
of my black robe
were only wider
I'd shelter all the people
in this up-and-down world

[941]

Mi wo sutete
yo wo sukuu hito mo
aru mono wo
kusa no ihori ni
hima motomu to wa

When there're
those who give their lives
trying to save others,
to hide in a grass hut
because I want a little leisure—

[539]

Awayuki no	The Three Thousand Worlds[1]
naka ni tachitaru	that step forth
michiōchi	with the light snow,
mata sono naka ni	and the light snow that falls
awayuki zo furu	in those Three Thousand Worlds

(Conch horns were blown by the farmers as a warning of danger.)

Ochikata yu	Again and again
shikiri ni kai no	from far off
oto su nari	the conches sound—
koyoi no ame ni	in tonight's rain
seki kuenamu ka[2]	will the dikes give way?

1. The universe.
2. Text in Yoshino Hideo's collection, p. 108; the poem is not included in the Tōgō Toyoharu edition.

(On receiving a gift of seven pomegranates)

[476]

Kakite tabe
tsumi saite tabe
warite tabe
sate sono nochi wa
kuchi mo hanatazu

Splitting them, eating
picking them apart, eating
breaking into them, eating—
after that never
letting them out of my mouth

[460]

Chimubaso ni
sake ni wasabi ni
tamawaru wa
haru wa sabishiku
araseji to nari

Dulse and wine
and wasabi—
with such gifts
my spring
can never be lonely!

[1040]

Yo no naka ni
majiranu to ni wa
aranedomo
hitori asobi zo
ware wa masareru

It's not that
I never mix
with men of the world—
but really I'd rather
amuse myself alone

[603]

Fukamigusa
ima wo sakari to
saki ni keri
taoru mo oshishi
taoranu mo oshi

Woody peonies
now just at the
best of their bloom—
too beautiful to pick
too beautiful not to pick

[1374]

Nomi shirami
ne ni naku aki no
mushi naraba
waga futokoro wa
Musashino no hara

Fleas, lice
any autumn bug that
wants to sing—
the breast of my robe
is Musashino moor![1]

[411]

Ōmiki wo
mitsuki itsutsuki
tabe einu
eite no nochi wa
matade tsugikeru

On three cups
five cups of
this fine wine I'm drunk—
and once drunk
I can pour for myself

1. Ryōkan is famous for taking the lice out of the breast of his robe, sunning them on a piece of paper on the veranda, and then carefully replacing them in his robe.

(Probably written at a dinner where he was served a vegetarian meal while the other guests ate wild fowl)

[1371]

Gan kamo wa
ware wo misutete
sari ni keri
tōfu ni hane no
naki zo ureshiki

The wild geese and ducks
have flown off
and left me—
I'm glad my bean curd
doesn't have wings!

[1359]

Ware dani mo
mada kuitaranu
shiragayu no
soko ni mo miyuru
kagebōshi kana

When even *I* haven't had
enough to eat,
at the bottom of my bowl
of rice gruel
my shadow hogging in!

[338]

Tori to moite
na uchi tamai so
misonou no
kaidō no mi wo
hami ni kitsureba

Don't take me for a bird
and pelt me
if I come
to eat the cherry-apples
growing in your garden!

[328]

Aki kaze ni
nabiku yamaji no
susuki no ho
mitsutsu ki ni keri
kimi ga iebe ni

In the fall breeze
bobbing by the mountain path,
plumes of pampas grass—
watching them, I've made my way
here to your house

[391]

Kaze wa kiyoshi   The breeze is fresh,
tsuki wa sayakeshi   the moonlight bright—
iza tomo ni   let's dance together
odori akasamu   the whole night through,
oi no nagori ni   a last memory for my old age

(Written to Teishin, 1830)

[244]

Azusa yumi   Now that catalpa-bowed [1]
haru ni narinaba   spring is here,
kusa no iho wo   leave your grass hut
toku dete kimase   hurry to me—
aitaki mono wo   I long to see you!

1. *makura-kotoba* or pillow word for "spring."

(Addressed to Teishin)

[316]

Mata mo koyo	Come again
shiba no ihori wo	if you don't mind
itowazuba	my hut of sticks,
susuki obana no	through dew-wet tails of pampas g‹
tsuyu wo wake wake	pushing pushing your way along

[235]

Koto shi areba	When you're busy
koto ari to iite	you send word you can't come
kimi wa kozu	because you're busy
koto shi naki toki wa	and when you're not busy
otozure mo nashi	you send no word at all

(Addressed to Teishin)

[291]

Itsu itsu to
machi ni shi hito wa
kitari keri
ima wa aimite
nani ka omowamu

When? when? I said
But the one I waited for
has come at last.
Seeing her now,
what more could I ask?

(Written in 1830)

[1336]

Misonou ni	These I grew in my garden:
ueshi akihagi	autumn bush clover,
hatasusuki	eulalia grass,
sumire tampopo	violets, dandelions,
nebu no hana	a silk tree in bloom,
bashō asagao	plantain, morning glory,
fujibakama	boneset,
shioni tsuyukusa	aster, spiderwort,
wasuregusa	day lilies—
asa na yū na ni	each morning, each evening
kokoro shite	taking pains to
mizu wo sosogite	pour on water,
hioi shite	rigging a sun shade,
sodateshinureba	nursing them along,
tsune yori mo	and just when I thought—
koto ni aware to	and others said too—
hito mo ii	they were
ware mo moishi wo	lovelier
toki koso are	than ever before,
satsuki no tsuki no	in the fifth month,
hatsuka mari	at twilight
itsuka no kure no	of the twenty-fifth day,
ōkaze no	that huge wind
kuruite fukeba	came howling like a fury,
aragane no	till they lay battered
tsuchi ni nukafushi	over the iron ground,
hisakata no	tangled by torrents

ame ni midarite	of rain from the sky,
momo chiji ni	till they'd been tumbled
momare ni kereba	a hundred thousand ways,
atarashi to	and all I could say was,
omou mono kara	how pitiful!
kaze no nasu	But because I know
waza ni shi areba	it's the work of the wind
semu sube mo nashi	I know there's nothing I can do

Envoy

[1337]

Waga yado ni	At my house
uete sodateshi	these hundred plants
momokusa wa	I planted and raised—
kaze no kokoro ni	only to give them up
makasu nari keri	to the will of the wind

[1079]

Sono kami wo
omoeba yume ka
utsutsu ka mo
yoru wa shigure no
ame wo kikitsutsu

Those old days—I wonder,
did I dream them
or were they real?
In the night I listen
to the autumn rain

The Pasania Nut Tree of Iyahiko

[1311]

Iyahiko no	Before the shrine
kami no mimae no	of Iyahiko,
shii no ki wa	the pasania nut tree—
ikuyo henuramu	how many years it's known,
kamiyo yori	from ages of the gods
kakushi aru rashi	always like this?
hotsue ni wa	Upper branches
teru hi wo kakushi	that shield the shining sun,
nakatsue wa	middle branches
kumo wo saegiri	barring the clouds,
shimotsue wa	lower branches
iraka ni kakari	that rest on roof tiles;
hisakata no	though frosts
shimo wa okedomo	fall from the sky,
tokoshie ni	it lives forever,
kaze wa fukedomo	though winds blow,
tokoshie ni	still it lives on,
kami no miyo yori	from holy ages
kakute koso	of the gods
ari ni kerashimo	ever like this,
Iyahiko no	the pasania nut
kami no mimae ni	that stands
tateru shii no ki	before Iyahiko Shrine

[1322]

Yukusa kusa	Each time I go
miredomo akanu	each time I come
Iwamuro no	looking at it but never tiring,
tanaka ni tateru	the lone pine that stands
hitotsu matsu no ki	in the field of Iwamuro

(For the parents of a dead child)

[1200]

Kainadete	You fondled him
oite hitashite	piggybacked him
chi fufumete	reared him, fed him the breast—
kyō wa kareno ni	and today bear him away
okuru nari keri	to the withered fields

(For the children who died in a smallpox epidemic; a *sedōka*)

[1182]

Haru sareba	When spring comes,
kigi no kozue ni	from every tree tip
hana wa sakedomo	the flowers will unfold,
momijiba no	but those fallen leaves
suginishi kora wa	of autumn, the children,
kaerazari keri	will never come again

(Written for Ryōkan's friend Abe Sadayoshi, whose eldest daughter had died. The poet speaks in the voice of the grieving father.)

[1206]

Shirayuki wa	White snow, heap up
chie ni furi shike	a thousand layers deep—
waga kado ni	the lost child
suginishi kora ga	will never come
kuru to iwanaku ni	to my gate again

(Written for a dying person)

[1243]

Gokuraku ni
waga chichi haha wa
owasuramu
kyō hizamoto e
iku to omoeba

My father and mother
in Paradise—
think of it,
today I go
to sit by their knees!

[1236]

Ryōkan ni
jisei aru ka to
hito towaba
Namu Amida Butsu
to iu to kotaeyo

If they ask
if Ryōkan has
some last words for the world,
tell them he says:
Namu Amida Butsu [1]

1. The ritual invocation of the Buddha Amida's name which, according to the teachings of the Jōdo and Shin sects, assures that the believer will be reborn in the Western Paradise of Amida.

(Written shortly before his death when he was suffering from severe
 diarrhea)

[183]

Koto ni idete
ieba yasukeshi
kudaribara
makoto sono mi wa
iya taegatashi

Putting it in words
it sounds
so simple
but with these runny bowels
my body is hard to bear!

KANSHI: Poems in Chinese

In High Spirits

[2]

Robe too short, jacket too long,
in high spirits, full of fight—that's how I get by.
On the road little boys suddenly spy me,
clap hands, all together give out with a *temari* song.[1]

1. A *temari* is a cloth ball wound with colored thread and used for various children's games, to which songs are sung.

Temari [1]

[6]

In my sleeve the colored ball worth a thousand in gold:
I dare say no one's as good at *temari* as me!
And if you ask what it's all about—
one—two—three—four—five—six—seven

1. The ball described in the preceding poem and the games, particularly counting games, played with it.

Grass Fight [1]

[3]

Again with the boys I fought a hundred grasses,
fought going, fought coming—what a brave fight we had!
Sun setting, lonely now, everyone gone home—
one round bright moon, whiter than autumn.

1. The "grass fight" is mentioned as early as T'ang times in China as a pas-
time played by girls on the fifth day of the fifth month, a genteel competition
of grasses or flowers which was imported to Japan and pursued under the
name *kusa-awase*. Ryōkan's grass fight, however, is a much more strenuous
affair in which the contestant selects tough weed stalks, loops them around
the stalks of his opponent, and conducts a tug-of-war.

[9]

Green spring, start of the second month,
colors of things turning fresh and new.
At this time I take my begging bowl,
in high spirits tramp the streets of town.
Little boys suddenly spot me,
delightedly come crowding around,
descend on me at the temple gate,
dragging on my arms, making steps slow.
I set my bowl on top of a white stone,
hang my alms bag on a green tree limb;
here we fight a hundred grasses,
here we hit the *temari* ball—
I'll hit, you do the singing!
Now I'll sing, your turn to hit!
We hit it going, hit it coming,
never knowing how the hours fly.
Passers-by turn, look at me and laugh,
"What makes you act like this?"
I duck my head, don't answer them—
I could speak but what's the use?
You want to know what's in my heart?
From the beginning, just this! just this!

[1]

Finished begging at the village crossroads,
now I stroll through the Hachiman Shrine
when children spot me, call to each other,
"That crazy monk from last year's back again!"

[15]

Breath of spring bit by bit milder;
rattling the rings on my staff, I head for the east town.
Green green, willows in the gardens;
bobbing bobbing, duckweed on the pond.
Alms bowl smelling sweet with rice from a thousand houses;
heart indifferent to ten-thousand-chariot glory.[1]
Following in tracks of old time Buddhas,
begging for food, I go my way.

1. The glory and wealth of a ruler with an army of ten thousand chariots; an old Chinese expression.

[16]

Time: first day of the eighth month; [1]
with begging bowl I enter the city streets.
A thousand gates unbolted in the dawn;
ten thousand homes where cooking smoke slants up.
Last night's rain washed the road clean;
autumn wind shakes the metal rings of my staff.
Taking my time, I go begging for food—
how wide, how boundless this Dharma world!

1. Under the lunar calendar New Year came in early February and autumn
comprised the seventh, eighth, and ninth lunar months.

Empty Begging Bowl

[21]

Blue sky, cold wild-geese crying;
empty hills, tree leaves whirling.
Sunset, road through a hazy village:
going home alone, carrying an empty bowl.

Summer, *Kansei* kasshi [1]

[246]

After Grain in Ear, dark and overcast,
black clouds lowering, never pulling apart:
swift lightning flickered all night,
rough winds blew the whole day through.
Flood waters crept over steps and stairs,
pouring rains drowned field and paddy.
In the village, no sound of children singing;
carts and horses set out but never came home.
The river waters raged and tumbled—
wherever you looked, banks wiped out.
Every commoner, young or old,
pressed into service, more weary with each day.
Ridges that bound the fields—where have they gone?
Hard to tell if the levees can be saved.
The young wife throws down her shuttle, comes running;
the old farmer leans on his spade and sighs.
What offerings of paper and cloth not proffered,
what god or spirit not implored?
But high Heaven is a mystery, hard to fathom—
enough to make you doubt if the Creator exists.
Who will haul the four conveyances,

1. There was no year with the cyclical designation *kasshi* in the Kansei era and commentators suggest that the title should read Bunka *kasshi,* which would correspond to 1804. Grain in Ear in the first line is a division of the solar year, ending around June 20, when the rainy season is at its height.

ensure the people a place of rest?[2]
I overheard the villagers talking:
"This year's grain crops did so well!
everyone working twice as hard as ever,
cold weather and warm coming right on time.
We plowed deep, weeded briskly,
off at dawn, at evening looking back—
And now in one morning the land laid waste—
what can we do but weep!"

2. Four types of vehicles used when the legendary Emperor Yü brought the flood waters of ancient China under control.

Done begging in a rundown village,
I make my way home past green boulders.
Late sun hides behind western peaks;
pale moonlight shines on the stream before me.
I wash my feet, climb up on a rock,
light incense, sit in meditation.
After all, I wear a monk's robe—
how could I spend the years doing nothing?

[137]

In the still night by the vacant window,
wrapped in monk's robe I sit in meditation,
navel and nostrils lined up straight,
ears paired to the slope of shoulders.[1]
Window whitens—the moon comes up;
rain's stopped, but drops go on dripping.
Wonderful—the mood of this moment—
distant, vast, known to me only!

1. This is the posture one is instructed to assume when practicing zazen or Zen style meditation. See Dōgen's instructions quoted in Heinrich Dumoulin, *A History of Zen Buddhism* (McGraw-Hill paperback, 1965), p. 161.

(The "you" of the poem is probably Ryōkan's close friend Abe
Sadayoshi (1779–1831), with whom he often exchanged poems.
Ryōkan is doing zazen in imitation of Bodhidharma, the founder of
the Zen sect.)

[321]

You've dropped the sutra scroll, head bowed in sleep;
I'm perched on my cushion, copying the old Founder.
Frog voices near and far sound incessantly;
the lamp glows and fades within the coarse-plaited blinds.

Visited by Thieves

[60]

My zazen platform, my cushion—they made off with both!
Thieves break into my grass hut, but who dares stop them?
All night I sit alone by the dark window,
soft rain pattering on the bamboo grove.

[47]

Dark of winter, eleventh month,
rain and snow slushing down;
a thousand hills all one color,
ten thousand paths where almost no one goes.
Past wanderings all turned to dreams;
grass gate, its leaves latched tight;
through the night I burn chips of wood,
quietly reading poems by men of long ago.

[27]

Shouldering firewood I climb down the green peak,
green peak where trails are never level.
Sometimes I rest under a tall pine,
listen quietly to the voice of spring birds.

As a boy I left my father, ran off to other lands,
tried hard to become a tiger—didn't even make it to cat!
If you ask what kind of man I am now,
just the same old Eizō I've always been.[1]

    1. Eizō was Ryōkan's name before he became a monk.

A Request for Rice

[50]

Bleak, bare, my three-span room;
a wreck, this creaky old body,
now especially in dark winter months—
I'd have trouble telling you all my ills.
Sipping gruel, I get through the cold night,
counting the days, waiting for sunny spring.
But if I don't ask for a measure of rice,
how can I last out the season?
Pondering, I came up with no workable plan,
so I write this poem, send it to you, old friend.

All my life too lazy to try to get ahead,
I leave everything to the truth of Heaven.
In my sack three measures of rice,
by the stove one bundle of sticks—
why ask who's got satori, who hasn't?
What would I know about that dust, fame and gain?
Rainy nights here in my thatched hut
I stick out my two legs any old way I please.

Rags and tatters, rags and tatters,
rags and tatters—that's my life.
Food—somehow I pick it up along the road;
my house—I let the weeds grow all around.
Watching the moon, I spend the whole night mumbling poems;
lost in blossoms, I never come home.
Since I left the temple that trained me,
this is the kind of lazy old horse I've become.

[59]

On peaks before, peaks behind, snow glinting white;
my grass gate shut tight, west of the rocky stream.
Through the long night in the fire pit I burn sticks of wood,
pulling on my beard, remembering times when I was young.

Long Winter Night

[69]

I remember when I was young
reading alone in the empty hall,
again and again refilling the lamp with oil,
never minding then how long the winter night was.

[73]

I lie alone in my grass hut,
all day not seeing a soul.
Alms bag—how long now it's hung on the wall,
walking stick left wholly to the dust.
Dreams wing away to mountain meadows;
waking, my spirit roams the city—
along the roadside, the little boys—
as always, they'll be waiting for me to come

[35]

Done with a long day's begging,
I head home, close the wicker door,
in the stove burn branches with the leaves still on them,
quietly reading Cold Mountain poems.
West wind blasts the night rain,
gust on gust drenching the thatch.
Now and then I stick out my legs, lie down—
what's there to think about, what's the worry?

[83]

First month of summer, Grain in Ear season[1]—
with a metal-ringed staff, alone I come and go.
Old farmers suddenly spy me,
drag me over to join their fun.
Woven rushes serve for our seats,
paulownia leaves take the place of plates.
A couple of rounds of wine in the field
and drunk, I doze off, head pillowed on the bank.

1. One of the divisions of the solar year, around June 6–20.

Dialogue in a Dream

[143]

Begging food, I went to the city,
on the road met a wise old man.
He asked me, "Master, what are you doing
living there among those white-clouded peaks?"
I asked him, "Sir, what are you doing
growing old in the middle of this red city dust?"
We were about to answer, but neither had spoken
when fifth-watch bells shattered my dream.

[65]

I have a walking stick—
don't know how many generations it's been handed down—
the bark peeled off long ago,
nothing left but a sturdy core.
In past years it tested the depth of a stream,
how many times clanged over steep rocky trails!
Now it leans against the east wall,
neglected, while the flowing years go by.

[168]

In a flash of lightning, sixty years;
world's glory and decay—clouds that come and go.
Deep night rains about to gouge out the foot of the cliff;
wick of the lamp glowing, guttering by the old window.

(In his later years, Ryōkan moved from his mountain hut to the Otogo Shrine at the southern foot of Mount Kugami, living there for the following ten years.)

[165]

As a boy I studied literature,
　　but was too lazy to become a Confucian;
in my young days I worked at Zen,
　　but got no Dharma worth handing down.
Now I've built a grass hut,
　　act as custodian of a Shinto shrine,
half a shrine man,
　　half a monk.

(Apparently written when Ryōkan happened to pass by his old mountain hut, the Gogō-an, some years after leaving it, and was shocked by its state of disrepair. It eventually fell to ruin, though it has since been rebuilt.)

[99]

This is the place I lived so long!
Alone with my lone staff I happened by—
wall fallen down, fox and rabbit runs;
well gone dry beside the tall bamboo.
Cobwebs in the window where I used to read,
dust coating my zazen platform,
fall weeds burying the steps in their tangle,
a cold cricket singing right in my face—
I pace back and forth, can't bear to leave,
desolate, staring into the evening sun.

[259]

How admirable—the fine gentleman,
in spare moments so often trying his hand at poetry!
His old-style verse is modeled on Han and Wei works;
for modern style, he makes the T'ang his teacher;
with what elegance shapes his compositions,
adding touches that are striking and new.
But since he never writes of things in the heart,
however many he may turn out, what's the point?

[185]

Buddha's something made up in the mind;
the Way—it doesn't exist either.
I'm telling you—believe what I say—
don't go off in some wild direction!
Point your cart shafts north and try to get to the tropics—
when do you think you'll ever arrive?

(The "twelve divisions" are the twelve sections into which the Buddhist scriptures are divided. The poem is an attack on the kind of sectarianism common in Chinese and Japanese Buddhism that seeks to exalt the verity and worth of one sutra over that of all the others.)

[187]

Buddha preached the twelve divisions,
each division full of purest truth.
East wind—rain comes in the night,
making all the forests fresh and new.
No sutra that does not save the living,
no branch in the forest not visited by spring.
Learn to understand the meaning in them,
don't try to decide which is "valid," which is not!

To Inscribe on a Picture of a Skull I Painted

[245]

All things born of causes end when causes run out;
but causes, what are they born of?
That very first cause—where did it come from?
At this point words fail me, workings of my mind go dead.
I took these words to the old woman in the house to the east;
the old woman in the house to the east was not pleased.
I questioned the old man in the house to the west;
the old man in the house to the west puckered his brow and
    walked away.
I tried writing the question on a biscuit, fed it to the dogs,
but even the dogs refused to bite.
Concluding that these must be unlucky words, a mere jumble
    of a query,
I rolled life and death into a pill, kneading them together,
and gave it to the skull in the meadowside.
Suddenly the skull came leaping up,
began to sing and dance for me,
a long song, ballad of the Three Ages,
a wonderful dance, postures of the Three Worlds.[1]
Three worlds, three ages, three times danced over—
"the moon sets on Ch'ang-an and its midnight bells."[2]

1. The three ages of past, present, and future; the three worlds of desire,
form, and formlessness.

2. The last line is taken verbatim from a poem entitled "For the Monk San-
tsang on His Return to the Western Regions," by the ninth century Chinese
poet Li Tung, translated in my *Chinese Lyricism* (New York: Columbia Univer-
sity Press, 1971), p. 120.

Drinking Wine with Yoshiyuki and Being Very Happy

(Yoshiyuki was Ryōkan's brother, four years his junior.)

[272]

Older and younger brother meet—
both with white eyebrows drooping down.
And what delight in this time of peace,
day after day getting drunk as fools!

When News of Saichi's Death Arrived

(Miwa Saichi was a *koji* or layman who studied Zen with Ryōkan until his death in the fifth month of 1807. To Ryōkan, who apparently had few other Zen students, his death was a great blow, and he referred to it often in his poems.)

[283]

Ah—my *koji!*
studied Zen with me twenty years.
You were the one who understood—
things I couldn't pass on to others.

I Dreamt of Saichi and Woke with a Feeling of Uneasiness

[291]

After twenty some years, one meeting with you,
gentle breeze, hazy moon, east of the country bridge:
we walked on and on, hand in hand, talking,
till we reached the Hachiman Shrine in your village of Yoita.

Paying Respects at the Grave
of My Teacher Shiyō

(Ōmori Shiyō (1738–1791), the Confucian scholar whose school in
Jizōdō by the Seba River Ryōkan attended as a boy. Shiyō
closed the school in 1777, shortly after Ryōkan began religious
training.)

[273]

Old grave on the side of a deserted hill
where year after year the sad grasses grow;
no one attending to sprinkle and sweep it,
only a reed-cutter at times passing by.
I remember long ago, hair in boy's braids,
going to school by the Seba River.
Then one morning we flew off in different directions;
after that no word from one another.
Now I've come home, and you've departed—
how can I face your spirit?
I pour a dipper of water over the stone,
a small gesture of respect for my teacher.
The bright sun suddenly sinks in the west;
in mountain fields, only the sound of pines.
Wandering back and forth, I can't bear to leave,
tears continually wetting my robe.

[369]

My one aim, to be a wandering monk,
how could I have lingered any longer?
Lugging a water jug, I took leave of my old teacher,
in high spirits set off for other parts,
mornings climbing to the top of the lone peak,
evenings crossing the dark sea's flow.
And while one word fails to match the Truth,
I vow all my life never to rest!

I remember when I was at Entsū-ji,
always sorry my way was such a solitary one.
Hauling firewood, I thought of Mr. P'ang;
treadling the pounder, I recalled old Lu.[1]
At *nisshitsu* I never dared to be last,
at morning *sanzen* always got there first.[2]
Since I left my place at the temple,
thirty long years have passed.
Mountains and seas lie between me and that land,
no one to bring me any news.
I think of the debt I owe my teacher, end in tears—
let them flow, flow to the river.

1. Mr. P'ang is the layman or *koji* P'ang, a devout Zen believer of T'ang times whose sayings have been preserved. Old Lu is Hui-neng, the famous Sixth Patriarch of Chinese Zen in the eighth century, who for a time worked at the temple pounding rice in a treadle-operated mortar.

2. *Nisshitsu* refers to the private interview between the Zen master and the student; *sanzen* here probably indicates the morning meditation period or some other morning ceremony.

Bothered by Something

[77]

I shaved my head, became a monk,
plowed through the weeds, spent years looking for the Way.
Yet now wherever I go they hand me paper and brush,
and all they say is "Write us a *waka!*" "Write us a Chinese
  poem!"

[30]

The plaintain before my window,
tall, lanky, brushing the clouds, cool:
writing *waka,* composing *kanshi,*
all day long I sit by its side.

Seventh Month, Sixteenth Day

[31]

Where to escape this steamy heat?
I like best the Izuruta Shrine.[1]
Miiin-miiin, the shrill of locusts fills my ears;
cool cool breezes come out of the wood.

1. A little local shrine at the village of Shimazaki, where Ryōkan lived shortly before his death.

ADMONITORY WORDS

EXCERPTS FROM Ryōkan's list of ninety *Kaigo* or "Admonitory Words," which seems to have been addressed mainly to himself. Several versions of the list exist; I follow that recorded in the *Hachisu no tsuyu*, Ōshima Kasoku, *Ryōkan zenshū* (Tokyo: Shingensha, 1958), pp. 526–28. The original is in Japanese.

Beware of:
  talking a great deal
  talking too fast
  volunteering information when not asked
  giving gratuitous advice
  talking up your own accomplishments
  breaking in before others have finished speaking
  trying to explain to others something you don't understand
    yourself
  starting on a new subject before you've finished with the
    last one
  insisting on getting in the last word
  making glib promises
  repeating yourself, as old people will do
  talking with your hands
  speaking in an affectedly offhand manner
  reporting in detail on affairs that have nothing to do with
    anything
  reporting on every single thing you see or hear
  making a point of using Chinese words and expressions

learning Kyoto speech and using it as though you'd known
   it all your life
speaking Edo dialect like a country hick
talk that smacks of the pedant
talk that smacks of the aesthete
talk that smacks of satori
talk that smacks of the tea master

According to the preface to the *Sōdōshū*, Ryōkan de-
clared there were three things he disliked:

poet's poetry
calligrapher's calligraphy
chef's cooking

STATEMENT ON BEGGING
FOR FOOD

THE RECEIVING OF GIFTS of food is the lifeblood of the Buddhist Order. For this reason we have our rituals for unwrapping gruel bowls and our rules for begging food. Vimalakīrti obtained "pure rice" from the Buddha of Fragrance Accumulated and offered it to the multitude that had gathered from all around; Chunda sought permission to present Shākyamuni with a final meal and received Shākyamuni's sanction.[1]

Long ago, when Prince Siddhārtha [Shākyamuni] was pursuing religious practices in the snowy mountains, he at first served under the ascetic Ālāra Kālāma and others, day after day eating no more than one hemp seed and one grain of wheat, observing the most difficult and painful austerities, but they were of no help to him in finding the Way. Then, realizing that they were not the correct method, he abandoned them and attained Enlightenment.

The observances of one Buddha shall be the observances for a thousand Buddhas. Thus we should understand that the Buddhas of the Three Worlds accepted gifts of food and at-

1. According to ch. 10 of the *Vimalakīrti Sutra*, Vimalakīrti through his magical powers obtained "pure rice," a kind of gruel made of rice cooked in milk and butter, from the Buddha mentioned above, and fed it to a vast multitude, yet the supply never ran out. Chunda, a humble blacksmith, presented a meal to Shākyamuni and his disciples that turned out to be Shākyamuni's last, since he grew ill and died as a consequence; however, he commended Chunda for the spirit in which the meal was offered. The text of the "Statement on Begging for Food" is found in Tōgō Toyoharu, *Ryōkan shishū*, pp. 421–28.

tained Enlightenment, and that the patriarchs and teachers down through the ages accepted food and transmitted the lamp of the Law.

Therefore it is said, "It is permissible to receive food that is properly offered, but it is not permissible to receive food that is impure." And again, "To eat large quantities of food will cause one to be drowsy and to sleep a great deal and will give rise to indolence and sloth; but to eat too little will leave one with no strength to practice the Way."

The *Sutra of the Buddha's Dying Instructions* says,[2] "You monks, you should look upon the receiving of food and drink as you would upon the taking of medicine, not increasing or decreasing the quantity because some of it tastes good to you and some tastes bad." And again, "Eat at fixed times and see that you live in cleanliness and purity. Work to free yourselves from delusion, and do not let the desire for much food destroy the heart of goodness within you. Be with yourselves like a wise man who gauges the amount of labor his ox can bear and never exhausts its strength by driving it beyond the limit."

The *Vimalakīrti Sutra* says, "Once Kāshyapa, moved by pity and compassion, purposely went to a poor village to beg for food.[3] But Vimalakīrti berated him, saying, 'Begging for food must be done in an equal-minded manner! Because we are equal-minded in matters of food, so we can be equal-minded in matters of the Dharma.' "[4]

2. The *Fo-ch'ui pan-nieh-p'an lüeh-shuo chiao-chieh ching* (*Busshi hatsunehan ryakusetsu kyōkai kyō*), a brief work of doubtful origin describing the Buddha's final hours and his dying instructions to his disciples; it is especially honored in the Zen sect.

3. Because by begging from the poor, he could give them an opportunity to gain religious merit.

4. Ryōkan summarizes the description of the incident from ch. 3 of the *Vimalakīrti Sutra*.

The *Rules for Zazen* says, "Not too cold in winter, not too hot in summer; if the room is too bright, lower the blinds; if it is too dark, slide open the window panels. Be moderate in food and drink and go to bed at a fixed hour."[5]

The "Formula on the Five Remembrances" says,[6] "First, I consider the effort that went into producing it. Second, I consider how it came into my hands. Third, I consider whether I have been diligent or neglectful in my own practice of virtue, and accept it accordingly. Fourth, I accept this food so that I may heal the decay of the body. Fifth, I accept it so that I may attain the Way."

All these writings attest to the importance of accepting gifts of food. If one accepts no food, then the body will not function smoothly. When the body does not function smoothly, the mind will not function smoothly; and when the mind does not function smoothly, it becomes difficult to practice the Way. Is this not why the Buddha is called a Jōgojōbu or one who "Controls Men Smoothly"?[7]

The men of ancient times said, "The mind of man is perilous, the mind of the Way is obscure. Only through concentration and oneness can you sincerely hold fast to the mean."[8]

To let the fingernails grow long and the hair become like a tangle of weeds, to go all year without bathing, now exposing the body to the burning sun, now refusing to eat the five

5. There are various formulations of the rules for zazen or Zen meditation. The quotation here resembles the rules laid down by Dōgen (1200–53), who has come to be regarded as the founder of the Sōtō branch of the Zen sect in Japan. Those who have done zazen in Japanese temples in winter may have had occasion to wonder just what the Zen definition of "too cold" may be.

6. A text recited by Zen practitioners before partaking of a meal.

7. One of the Jūgō or Ten Epithets of the Buddha.

8. A celebrated passage from the "Pronouncement of the Great Yü," a section of the Confucian *Book of Documents*.

grains—these are the ways of the six teachers of heretical doctrines.[9] They are not the ways of the Buddha. And practices that resemble these, even though they may not be the same, one should recognize as the ways of heretical doctrines, unworthy to be trusted and followed.

In general, to remove oneself from the doting involved with kin and family, to sit upright in a grass hut, to circle about beneath the trees, to be a friend to the voice of the brook and the hue of the hills[10]—these are the practices adopted by the ancient sages and the model for ages to come.

I once heard an old man say that, because many of the monks of former ages used to hide themselves away in the deep mountains and remote valleys, they were far removed from human settlements and constantly encountered difficulties in begging for food. At times they had to gather mountain fruits or pick wild greens in order to provide themselves with enough to eat.

Nowadays we have our Mokujiki practitioners who, though they reside in the communities where others live, make a point of refusing to eat the five grains.[11] What kind of practice is this? It resembles Buddhist ways but is not really Buddhist; it resembles the austerities of the heretical teachers but is not really heterodox. Would we be justified in saying that such

9. Six religious and philosophical leaders who lived at the time of Shākya-muni and advocated severe ascetic practices.

10. An allusion to the famous lines in Su Tung-p'o's so-called enlightenment verse ("Presented to the Chief Abbot of Tung-lin Temple"):

The voice of the brook is the eloquent tongue of Buddha;
the hue of the hills—is it not his pure form?

11. Mokujiki or "tree-eater," as the name indicates, means one who lives exclusively on the fruits and nuts of trees. There were several well-known Japanese monks who followed this practice, the most famous being the Shingon monk Mokujiki Ōgo (1536–1608).

men are parading their eccentricity and leading the populace astray? If not, then we must suppose them to be quite mad and intoxicated with the Buddhist Law. The people of the time pay them great reverence, looking on them as arhats possessed of all the six supernatural powers, and they themselves, because of the persistent reverence paid them by others, come to believe that their own way is vastly superior. What a spectacle, what a spectacle! One blind man leading a multitude of the blind—soon they will tumble into a great pit!

When the men of old sacrificed themselves for the sake of the Dharma, they rid themselves of all ego, never greedy for fame or gain, seeking the Way alone. Therefore the heavenly beings bestowed alms upon them and the dragon spirits looked up to them. But the men of today claim they are carrying out practices difficult to practice, enduring deprivations difficult to endure, and yet all they are doing is needlessly wearying the body given them at birth by their father and mother. What a waste, what a waste! It is of course not right to try to cling to life and limb at all cost. But deliberately to place them in peril—how could that be right either? To go too far is as bad as not going far enough.[12]

As a matter of fact, I know that there is nothing difficult about endangering the body; the difficult thing is to keep it constantly whole and well. Therefore I say, the most difficult thing of all is to preserve continuity.[13] In all due respect I write these words for those who are practicing the Way, so that they may consider them wisely and make their choice.

The Shramana Ryōkan

12. The last sentence is quoted from the Confucian *Analects* XI, 15.
13. Ryōkan probably means in particular the continuity of the religious teachings handed down from the Zen masters of the past.

Translations from the Oriental Classics

Studies in Oriental Culture

Companions To Asian Studies

Introduction To Oriental Civilizations

Wm. Theodore de Bary, *Editor*